SCATALOG

The #2 Bestseller!

A Compendium of Mail Ordure Delights

BALLOON KNOT PRODUCTIONS

Illustrations by Gary Hallgren

T0113750

SIMON & SCHUSTER

NEW YORK LONDON TORONTO SYDNEY SINGAPORE

Simon & Schuster
Rockefeller Center
1230 Avenue of the Americas
New York, NY 10020

Simon & Schuster and colophon are registered
trademarks of Simon & Schuster, Inc.

For information about special discounts for bulk purchases,
please contact Simon & Schuster Special Sales:
1-800-456-6798 or business@simonandschuster.com.

Book design by Charles Kreloff

Manufactured in the United States of America
10 9 8 7 6 5 4 3 2 1

Library of Congress Cataloging-in-Publication Data is available.

ISBN 978-0-7432-3536-5

INTRODUCTION

Money is like manure, of very little use except it be spread.

—Sir Francis Bacon, *Essays*

And in the end the age was handed
The sort of shit that it demanded.

—Ernest Hemingway, "The Age Demanded"

I f you're living right, it happens every day. One by one, they're squeezed through that narrow slot and fall with a series of satisfying sloppy splats and comforting heavy thuds.

Oh, we may speak of them—if we speak of them at all—with our noses turned up. But how necessary they are! And what private, personal pleasure they bring!

We refer, obviously, to mail order catalogs—the way America does its business!

It was the eminent philosopher George Carlin who first observed that one's own possessions are referred to as "my stuff," while other peoples' property is known as "your shit." It follows that, as we exchange commodities, we are selling our shit (marketed as "stuff") while acquiring in turn, what we believe to be "stuff " (but which is, in fact, only other people's shit).

It is usually assumed that the prefix "scat-"—as in "scatology" or "scatophageous"—is derived from *skato*, the Greek word for excrement. But were you to consult the *Oxford English Dictionary* as to the meaning of the word "scat," you would discover that it is there defined as "treasure, money."

The ancient Mayans called gold "the excrement of the gods," and the apostle Paul referred to currency as "filthy lucre" (I Timothy 3:8). But it was Sigmund Freud (in *Character and Anal Erotism*, 1908) who first made the explicit connection between the love of feces and the love of money—and, by extension, to the spirit of capitalism—which is to say, the overwhelming urge to find oneself "rolling in it."

The ever-so-slight difference between money and shit was observed by the Emperor Vespian (A.D. 69-79) who observed, while collecting the coins from the pay toilets he had installed all over Rome, *"Pecunia non olet"*—that is, "Money doesn't stink."

Consider the simple elegance of our zero-sum efficient economic system. First we consume, then we produce, then we consume what we produce—in a cycle of consumption and production that leaves us all with shit-eating grins on our faces!

And mail order catalogs play a vital role in this process. They put—so to speak—the "gross" in "gross national product."

Scatalog: The #2 Bestseller! is an anthology: a collection of our all-time favorite catalogs. They may differ in style, from smarmy sweet talk to screaming hard sell—but each of them has the same vital message: "DEAR SIR OR MADAM, BUY OUR SHIT!"

> *Property remains excremental, and is known to be excremental in our secret hearts, the unconscious. Jokes and folklore…the wisdom of folly, tell the secret truth. The assimilation of money with excrement does not render money valueless. On the contrary, it is the path whereby extraneous things acquire significance of the human body, and hence value. If money were not excrement, it would be valueless.*

—Norman O. Brown, *Life Against Death*

Contents

The Crapper Image A very upmarket catalog, of the kind usually found tucked into seatback pockets on airplanes. It may be distinguished from the adjacent sick-bag by the pictures it contains—goofy white people grinning at shiny, expensive luxury gadgets, executive toys, last-minute gifts, and nifty, battery-operated devices for performing intimate operations you've never even considered doing by hand.

W. C. Pooterman A frankly pretentious little catalog, offering a selection of faux-historical items, chiefly of apparel. Exotic climes and romantic times are evoked, to inspire you with nostalgia for places you've never been and for someone else's past—all in deep-purple, tourist-baiting prose.

When Nature Calls Whether you're just taking your allergies for a nice brisk walk in the country or actually planning to slaughter some unsuspecting fellow creature, this catalog offers a variety of rustic but trendy survival gear—all the comforts of home in the Great Outdoors.

Toylets 'R' Us What can you get for the child who has everything? More of it! Thousands of breakable, loseable plastic items, desirable movie tie-ins, ridiculously expensive advanced robotics, as well as some of that educational Swedish handmade stuff kids hate.

The Potty Barn Knickknacks, flatware, and furniture for haute yuppies. Everything that today's young "nesters" require to further foul their nests.

USHITA A catalog of tasteless novelties, cheap T-shirts with creepy slogans, and highly impractical practical jokes—possibly not all of them made in America.

 EFFLUVIA New Age spirituality. Many allegedly hand-crafted items of a whimsical, organic, suburban-bohemian, high-colonic, holistic nature.

 Modern Manurity A plethora of products to meet the quavering but constant demands of the nation's fastest-growing (while, paradoxically, shrinking) demographic—old farts.

 SWEET SMELL OF SUCCESS All the glittering prizes—an array of corporate tchotchkes, including mottoes, employee awards, and traveling salesmen's "leave behinds."

 BOWELS & NOBOWL The best of great literature and popular writing, available on videotape, audiotape, CD, DVD—even, every so often, in "book" form.

 NATIONAL MUSEUM O'FART A collection of tasteful middlebrow reproductions, calendars, date books, paperweights, and just plain cultural accessories, for PBS watchers and those of us who much prefer museum gift shops to the adjacent museums.

 **THE CABINET OF COPRO-COLLECTIBLES** Turn your casual interest into a hobby. Transform your hobby into an obsession. We can deliver to your home (no CODs, please!) a variety of fake antiques, forged documents, bogus sports memorabilia, and museum-quality knockoffs.

SCATALOG

THE CRAPPER IMAGE

NEVER WIPE AGAIN!

In your active "get up and go" lifestyle, you want to "go and get up!" You don't have precious time to fritter away wiping your ass. Now, thanks to Stealth Wipe®, your ass-wiping days are behind you! The hi-tech, hands-free Stealth-Wipe® device uses GNP (Global Navigation Positioning system) technology, first developed by U.S. Navy rear admirals for swabbing the poop deck, to "search and destroy" every trace of you-know-what from you-know-where! With fail-safe DD® (Defecation Detection) by our orbiting "brown eye in the sky" satellite, and laser-powered DES® (Dirty End of the Stick).

THE E-Z MAKE-A-MESH® HAMMOCK

At last! With its built-in "honey bucket," it's the hammock you never have to leave! Now you can make a movement without making a move! Perfect for those lazy-hazy, "take a load off" days of summer! So let yourself go! Easy does it with E-Z® ! It's "re-laxative"!

HOW DO YOU DOO?

How often have you thought, "Wow! I must have lost five pounds!"? Or looked back and said, "That one must be at least a foot!"? Now you can know for sure! This attractive, easy-to-install Waste Measurement System® includes a highly sensitive, waterproof Gross Weight® scale and a precisely calibrated Yard Shtick®, as well as an easy-to-apply, in-bowl Flop-Flap® counter. Large, easy-to-read LED display. Wall mount included. (Also available in metric.)

WHAT DO YOU CALL A SUPER-DOOPER POOTER SCOOTER?

It's the ultimate in personal transport—The Razzer®, from Crapper Image! You're sure to feel the wind at your back, because the miniature motor (engineered by Fahrtschnell of Munich) is powered by methane, your very own "natural gas"!

HOW DOES YOUR GARDEN GROW?

A Crapper Image Exclusive! The Dungarama® Home Fertilizer System
At the touch of a button, powerful vacuum tubes from your toilet spray a mist of your precious personal organic fertilizer directly over your front lawn, or onto your backyard flowerbeds!

WORLD'S SMALLEST TOILET®

Incredible, but true! It's fully functional, yet fits in the palm of your hand!

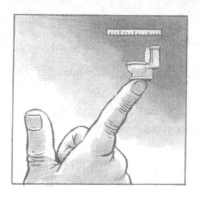

THE POO PUTTER®

It's a plunger! It's a putter! Now you can practice your two favorite "pastimes" at the same time!

SHARE A SCAT WITH YOUR FAVORITE CAT!

Litter Box For Two®

A "purr-fect," hyper-hygienic opportunity to share "quality time" with your beloved kitty. Pet owners agree— it's nothing to sniff at!

5

SOOTHE YOUR SENSES WITH THIS DECORATIVE CRAPQUARIUM®

An ever-changing underwater world of dozens of colorful, bobbing "floaters" and swirling "sinkers," which scientists tell us reduce stress. Your choice of soothing, amusing environments, such as "East River" (with "Vito" in cement overshoes), the "Raw Sewage Kaleidoscope," the humorous "Bubble Butt," and "The Lost Incontinence of Atlantis."

DISCOBOWL®

Let yourself Go-Go-Go! Shake your booty while you do your duty! Do the "bump" while you take a dump! Feel the beat beneath your seat! Utilizes patented "bottom woofer" and "strobe-seat" technology to get you moving to such disco classics as "I Like to Do It" by KC and the Sunshine Band, Donna Summer's "I Feel Love," and the Trammps' "Where the Happy People Go."

TAILS, YOU WIN®

"Just gas"—or is it? For those moments when you feel the urge—but you're not sure exactly what's "coming down the pike"—here's a coin to flip before you let 'er rip.

"BUCKET" SEATS®
FOR YOUR SPORTS CAR!

Because, when you're out for a spin in your costly roadster, shabby, grubby service station "facilities" just aren't for you!

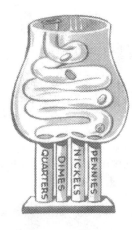

BUTT BANK®

When the British go to use the "loo," they say they're off to "spend a penny." Install this clever, educational Butt Bank® in your executive washroom, and "make a deposit" each time you "make a deposit!" It won't be long before you're feeling "flush"!

EXECUTIVE TIME-SAVER®

The ultimate in efficiency for the executive on the go! A portable, Auto-kathartik® Robot who eats your food for you, digests it for you, even excretes it for you! Add-on accessories allow you to shit, shave, shower, and shampoo—simultaneously!

THEY'LL SAY, "HE MAKES A PILE!"

A 14-foot Inflatable Doo-Pile Lawn Ornament®
A whimsical monument to your personal productivity! It's sure to get the neighbors talking about how much you make!

DINGLEBERRY PICKER®

Why worry about those hard-to-eliminate "will-knots"? This simple, portable device attaches easily to the bottom of any toilet seat, and employs space-age Phazer® technology for dealing with pesky "klingons."

20/20 HINDSIGHT®

Digitalize the experience! Miniaturized in-bowl video Crap-Corder® camera keeps you up-to-the minute on how you're doin' "back there." With optional "brown-eye" reduction filter.

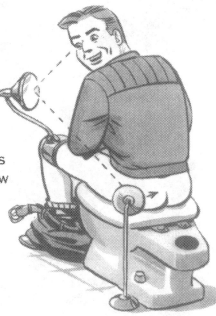

9

CRAPPER IMAGE PRODUCTS FOR THE HOME ORIFICE

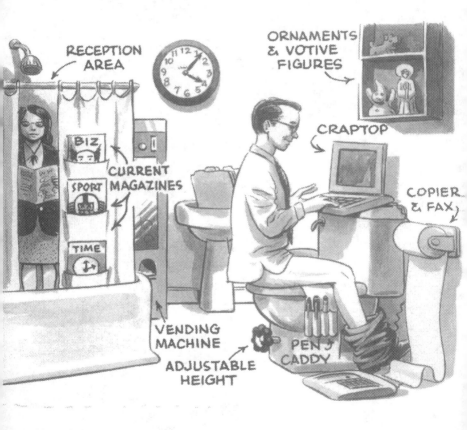

RECEPTION AREA

ORNAMENTS & VOTIVE FIGURES

CRAPTOP

BIZ

SPORT

CURRENT MAGAZINES

TIME

COPIER & FAX

VENDING MACHINE

ADJUSTABLE HEIGHT

PEN CADDY

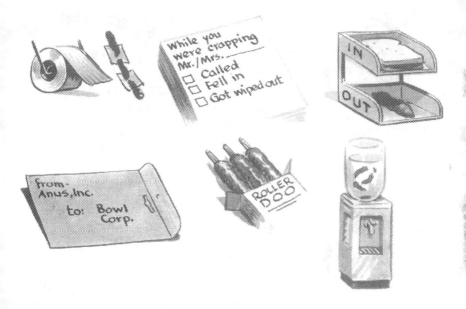

Do your business while you do your business! It's your "Inner Sanctum," a private place, where you can bear down hard, or just sit and think. It's your personal space, that room in your home with a lock on the door and an atmosphere all its own. Guaranteed to increase your productivity, until you're feeling flush! Our powerful BM Craptop® computer lets you input while you output. With Re-Lax® Inside, for faster downloading and logging out. Hands-free Throne-phone® with "brown-noise" filter muffles the "ca-cacophany." Soft, strong two-ply Fax-TP® fax paper dispenser. Can't work it out with a pencil? Our Auto-kathartik® software can help you to "budge it."

THE SILENT BUTTLER®

Strictly for gentlemen and ladies of de-stinktion: The Silent Buttler®! The ultimate *après-merde* accessory.

EXEC-O-LAV®

You travel first class. Why shouldn't your ass? You're finally in the air, cell phone activated, PalmPilot at the ready, when you feel "that" urge. No need to stand in the aisle with the hoi polloi, dodging the beverage cart, watching that interminable "occupied" sign. Because, savvy business traveler that you are, you've brought Crapper Image's Exec-O-Lav® on board!

SMELLAPHONE!®

Based on our original Smellaphone® technology, Crapper Image now proudly introduces the portable Smellaphone!®

BUNG-O-MATIC® FLATULENCE FILTER

Is your breath fresh—at BOTH ENDS? Now you can banish forever that socially unaccept- able phenomenon doctors call "hole-itosis," with our state-of-the-fart Bung-O-Matic® Flatulence Filter! With streamlined "bullet head" design for easy insertion, the Bung-O-Matic® contains thousands of charcoal granules, which absorb any and all noxious "rotten egg" odors. And, once firmly in place, the Bung-O-Matic® also prevents that unpleasant rectal experience commonly known as "turtle head." The Bung-o-Matic® is also available with our exclusive Frapp-No-Mo® Acoustic Adapter, which converts embarrassing "raspberry" noises to a sound well pitched beyond the range of human ear.*

*Should not be used in the vicinity of dogs or fine crystal.

BIG BROWN FLOATER®

Stink or swim, you'll have the pool to yourself this summer when you splash in aboard our inflatable Big Brown Floater®!

SWIRLY®

Swarms of flies, ants, and other pesky insects won't spoil YOUR outdoor picnic or barbecue fun this summer! Not if you have a Crapper Image Swirly® somewhere in your backyard! This amazing, all-natural product draws flies, bugs, and other pesky creatures like magic! Each Swirly® comes sealed in its own foil wrapper. Before your patio party gets underway, briefly microwave a Swirly®, unwrap it, place it discreetly in a faraway corner, and ENJOY!

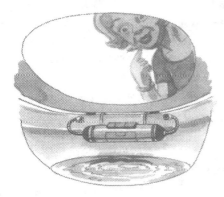

LASER-POWERED LOAF PINCHER®

Has that high-fiber diet you're on got you lowering coils too big for any bowl? Don't call the plumber! Let our battery-operated Loaf Pincher® cut that monster lunker down to flushable size!

FANNY PACK FART RECORDER®

Our exclusive, miniature, professional-grade directional Rear-Ear® microphone is the secret to fail-safe, distortion-free recordings of every performance of your personal "classical gas." Scent-sensitive® digital technology even records your "silent but deadly" efforts!

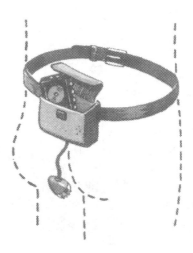

EVAK-U-JAK®

Blocked? Bound? Plugged-up? Dose yourself no more with foul-tasting laxatives that invariably go to work when it's most inconvenient. Get yourself "moving" with Evak-U-Jak® , the easy-to-use and fast-acting atomic-powered enema system. For your convenience, each Evak-U-Jak® comes with a month's supply of lead-lined Krappy Saks® (please dispose of nuclear waste thoughtfully).

THE LBJ®

Like many an executive, your busy schedule demands that you sometimes make—or take—a call while answering "nature's call." Our exclusive Husher® bathroom phone muffler system is programmed to eliminate potentially embarrassing "brown noise"—the sounds of grunts, splashes, and sighs—so the party on the other end need never know what's going on at your end!

W. C. POOTERMAN

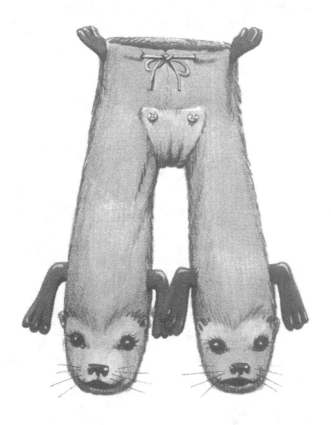

Sealskin Guano Harvesters' Pantaloons

When you find yourself downwind of a vast herd of reeking, rutting bachelor seals, chances are you're on the barren, godforsaken Lobos Islands, off the coast of Peru, where the undernourished but fashion-forward natives eke out a difficult existence by collecting the potassium-rich guano with which the blubbery sea creatures liberally daub the rocky shores. To a man, the guano harvesters wear these distinctive trousers, which they fashion out of the hides of seals—partly to camouflage themselves as they scamper amongst the herds, and partly out of pure spite.

Eau de Paris

This is toilet water that really *is* toilet water, bottled at source, directly beneath one of the picturesque wrought-iron Art Nouveau *pissoirs* in the 18th Arrondissement. The semi-clear, slightly amber liquid is redolent of the vintage Champagne recently consumed by local gourmets—with perhaps just a hint of escargot.

Colonel Blimp's Thunderbox

In 1915, on the Western Front, the orders came down from HQ. It was time for "the Big Push," and England expected every man to do his duty. And, by jingo, every serving British officer did his duty—and he did it in his very own "Thunderbox." We have painstakingly reproduced a limited number of these museum-quality seats-of-ease. Says one satisfied buyer, "To use one is to travel back in time and experience a gas attack on the Somme."

Affordable, classic Reproduction Toilet Tissue (from R. Swyppe & Co.)

"Fortune's close-stool to give to a nobleman!"
—Shakespeare, *All's Well That Ends Well* v. ii. 17-18

The Rustic, reproduced from Sears Roebuck catalog pages

The Greatest Generation, portraits of Hitler or Tojo

The Die-Hard Democrat

The True Blue Republican

The Dixie Special

Enron Stock Certificates

British Museum-quality toilet paper, with sandpaper finish

The "Tail Wind Tommy" Bomber Jacket

Heroic young Marine pilot George Herbert Walker Bush would have been "in deep doo-doo" indeed if he hadn't been wearing one of these when flying his missions over enemy territory! Tailored to stop right at the belt line, these fleece-lined leather jackets were designed to allow our WWII fighter pilots to "let fly!" in full, furious flight. Clad in these stylish "bum freezer" jackets, the Greatest Generation dropped their payloads all over the world.

Diaper-Kyfah

"I like the desert," said T. E. Lawrence, "because it's clean."
And this is how he kept it that way, with his personal
adaptation of the traditional Bedouin head scarf. Made of
soft, absorbent Egyptian cotton from M&M Enterprises.
Travelers to the Middle East are invariably impressed by the
fastidiousness of the natives in matters of personal hygiene.
Although they have the barren, sandy wastes of the entire
Sahara at their disposal—an area you and I might think of as
a gigantic litter box—they prefer, whenever possible, to utilize
indoor "facilities." An ancient Moroccan once disclosed to me
that the reason "everyone came to Rick's Place" was that
Rick's Place had the only working toilet in Casablanca!

Gaz De Napoleon

All the world knows that the French have a distinctive air about them. What is their secret? Legend has it that this popular *cologne pour les hommes* had its origins when one Jacques Merdeux, a humble foot soldier at the battle of Austerlitz, was quick-witted enough to capture and preserve a cloud of Napoleon's aromatic flatulence, emitted at the very moment when the famously constipated Emperor gave the order to advance.

Yak Dung Kindling

The fabled Italian explorer Marco Polo returned from the mysterious East with indelible memories of "Yuk," the traditional "firewood" of nomadic Tibetan yak herders. An entry in his journal reads, "Dey herda da yaks, dey live ina da yurts, dey eata da yogurt an' dey burna da yuk." Now chunks of this highly combustible, organic substance are available for the American home hearth. Like Marco, you will never get the pungent aroma out of your mind—or your clothes.

So That's Why They Called It a "Bowler"!

What could be more distressing to a man about town than to discover—having heeded the call of nature—that the facility in which he finds himself contains only a meager offering of coarse and uncouth toilet tissue—or, worse yet, no toilet tissue at all? Fashionable gentlemen of a finer, wiser time were never thus nonplussed, for they had access to a bountiful supply of soft, luxurious TP, which they discreetly carried with them, beneath their stylish "bowler" hats. And we have it on the authority of a distinguished British toff (now retired) that upon occasion the (entirely waterproof) hat itself may serve as an emergency commode!

No More "Logjams"!

It was in the dusty window of a quaint antique toy shop in Bremen that we spotted this cunning example of German workmanship—a clockwork *Holzfaller*, or lumberjack, intended to be wound up and then lowered into a toilet bowl, where, with his swinging ax, he breaks up the "logjams" which are the invariable consequence of a *Strudel und Schnitzel* diet. If you're a lover of fine cheeses—and who isn't?—you're sure to find plenty of use for this adorable little "shit-disturber."

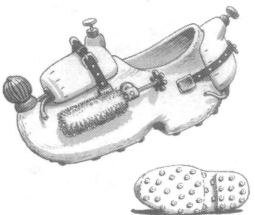

Parisian Walking Shoes

How, one has often asked oneself—while scraping the mal-odorous doggy-doo out of the treads of one's sneakers—do the ever-so-chic Parisians themselves keep the *merde* off their *chaussiers*? The answer, it appears, is that when walking their pets they always wear these cunning, if unglamorous, self-cleaning "anti-*crotte sabots*."

Our intrepid founder, W. C. Pooterman, invites you to join him on a 21-day Magical Dysentary Tour!

An excretory expedition of intercontinental incontinence, as we back-door trot our way from the domain of Delhibelly to the land of Montezuma's revenge and the Aztec two-step! See the Lurkies, the Scatters, the Scoots, the Runs, the Fluzes, and Dia Rio.

29

It is with deepest regret that we must inform you that this is the last W. C. Pooterman catalog you will ever receive.

An unforeseen change in America's habits of consumption first caused our production to slow to a trickle, and has finally resulted in the closing of all our U.S. outlets.

Pooterman will continue its international operations, in Assoule, Morocco; Shitang, Republic of China; Shitara, Japan; Crappone-sur-Arzon, France; Poopo, Bolivia; Turdera, Argentina; Dunga Bunga, Pakistan; Fartura, Brazil; and Dududu, South Africa.

When Nature Calls

Oh, we take no cathartic
  in weather so Arctic;
A trip to the toilet's a toil
  for the bold;
With far outdoor plumbing
  and cold so benumbing,
We find it much better to
  have and to hold.
          —Anon.

Cookin' with Gas

No more boring firewood gathering! This handy camp stove utilizes your own "natural gas." Cook tonight's pork and beans with last night's pork and beans.

The Complete Turd-Watcher's Field Guide

How to tell a meadow muffin from a buffalo chip, a horse apple from a cow pie! With bonus scratch 'n' sniff insert.

Turd Dogs of the World

A portfolio of classic canine portraits by noted animal artist Dougie Pyle: the Lavator Retriever, the Westphalian Pottie Pointer, and the Irish Turdier.

Does a Bear Shit in the Woods?

Exclusive to When Nature Calls. A series of limited edition bronzes: *Big Game of North America and Their Spoor!* These masterfeces of wildlife sculpture portray nature's most majestic creatures in the act of dumping. Actual-size reproductions of their excreta add total authenticity!

All-Weather Windbreakers

The ultimate in outdoor wear, with patented "trapdoor" backflap and optional "duck call" accessory.

Basket o'Leaves

For the times when you find yourself having to use indoor plumbing. Every handful is guaranteed to give you that rough 'n' ready outdoor feeling!

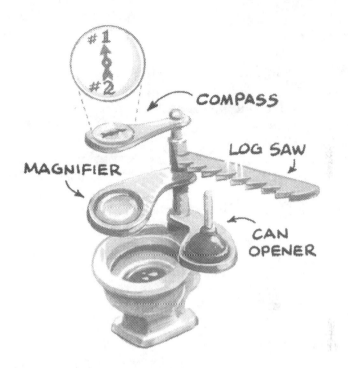

COMPASS

LOG SAW

MAGNIFIER

CAN OPENER

Swiss Army Toilet

Don't go into the woods without one. It's rustproof and portable, and comes complete with can opener, tweezers, log saw, compass, and magnifying glass.

Trophy Mounts

Let Dooley's Taxidermists of Bangor immortalize your lunker!

Shit Gun

NEW! Our fully loaded, double-barreled, pump-action *Shit Gun!* You'll never again be "out of ammo" just when you want to "squeeze off another round."

Poop Tent

Thanks to *Poop Tent,* our lightweight, pop-up, personal latrine, there's no need to be "caught with your pants down" on the trail. Lets you "lower a log" in peace and privacy, away from the prying eyes of your hiking buddies and other prurient fauna.

The Hook, Line and Stinker

The *Hook, Line and Stinker* home-fishing kit lets you reel in all "the big ones" that used to "get away" by re-creating your favorite fishin' hole in your toilet. You can choose to proudly display your catch of brown trout, crappies and grunts, or "release, catch, and release." (Hold the flush handle down for that "sport fishing" experience).

Shit Kickers

Attention, hikers! When walking the Appalachian Trail, you'll look like a local in your waterproof, steel-toed *Shit Kicker* boots!

For Xtreme sports enthusiasts only!

At the critical moment, the "breakaway" seat of our stylish and practical *Para-shite* pants releases the load of doo-doo that is always there.

Why skate board when you can Scat Board?

Skidmarks guaranteed!

(When in Maine, visit our facilities.)

Play-Doo

Hours of hands-on fun—the kind kids like! Play-doo comes in 5 great, semiwashable Crapola shades of brown, from Preemie yellow to Prune Juice black. Comes with the Play-doo Squeezie—they giggle like crazy at that rude, wet sound!

Shat-a-pult

Kids love to "let it fly!" with the educational, historical Shat-a-pult! As actually used in battle by ancient armies! Comes complete with washable cardboard medieval outhouse for use as target.

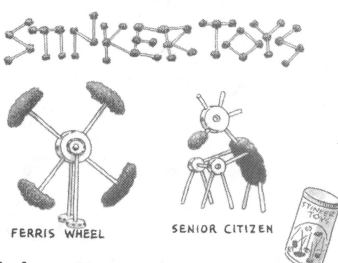

FERRIS WHEEL   SENIOR CITIZEN

Stinker Toys

Kids connect colorful wooden sticks and wheels to their very own feces for hours of old-fashioned fun! Plus: All the parts kids need to make "Doo-man the Hu-man!" Deluxe set includes electric motor. Educator approved. "I approve of the way children get involved in making the primary components of this toy by using the products of their own digestive systems."—a leading educator

Cacky

Our most popular pull toy ever! Big 6-inch doody-lump on a string, makes incongruous quacking sound as it rolls along on colorful wheels.

QUACK!

QUACK!

The Happy Potty®
Toilet Troll

New!!! The Happy Potty® Toilet Troll—Inflatable ten-foot "monster" that pops up right at potty time! Sure to scare the crap out of any child!

Time for a change?

Now it's easy to know—using our handy Diaper Dipstick!

43

Stincoln Logs®

Back by popular demand. The classic rustic frontier craphouse-building kit.

Grunty Dump Truck and Jammies

Kids are sure to "shit a brick" when they ride this toy. It's Grunty the Happy Dump Truck™ as seen on TV. At bedtime kids love to dress up as their TV cartoon favorite, Grunty the Happy Dump Truck™. And Grunty never has "an accident," thanks to the convienient "trapdoor" in back!

Little Susie Squirt

At last! The doll you can give an enema to! She talks! "Mommy, I'm constipated!" Just fill the bag with chocolate syrup and insert. After her enema, Susie makes in your milk!

Stinkin' Center Poopet Theater

Everything you need to put on a show! Poopets, two-ply TP curtains, programs, tickets.

Whoopsie-Land®

NEW! It's Whoopsie-Land! Make potty training fun by turning your home toilet into an amusement park!

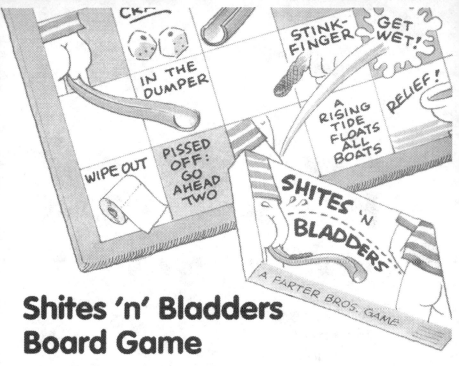

Shites 'n' Bladders
Board Game

NEW! It's wet and wild! It's down and dirty! It's the classic potty-training board game that's pant loads of fun for the whole family.

Mister Shit Head

No more wasted potatoes!

From our Toylets 'R' Us Book Nook—paper you can use so many ways!

CLASSICS from our BACK LIST

The Brownstain Bears

Black Beauty II

Breaking Wind in the Willows

Little Loo-loo

The Little Outhouse on the Prairie

Spot on the New Carpet

The Adventures of Doctor Dooplenty

Tintin dans le Merde

Oops! Katy Did It Again

Winnie Goes Pooh

What's Brown and Sounds Like a Bell? And Other Favorite Riddles

Honey Wagon

NEW! Let the good times roll!

Musical Movement Mobile

Free-form lumpy shapes swirl over baby's head to timeless toidy tunes like, "The Poop in the Potty Goes Round and Round" and "If You're Crappy and You Know It, Wash Your Hands."

Inflatable Cess Pool

Calling all party-poopers! Make a big splash in your own backyard!

THE POTTY BARN

A Cornucopia of Commodious Commodes

"If you don't shop here, you don't know squat!"

The Right Regal Throne

Because your home is your castle.

The Honeymooner

An intimate, romantic two-seater for loving couples.

The 007

The ingenious, irascible M couldn't have come up with a higher-tech "Spy Can"—it comes complete with an emergency ejector seat.

The Lazy-Bowl

Easy does it! This comfy recliner model lets you take a load off while you drop a load.

The Asstonaut

No problem, Houston! A space-age antigravity model for your every blast off.

The Piano Stool

For music lovers only.

The Rustic

Our no-frills, nostalgic model comes complete with a vintage Sears Roebuck catalog.

The Presidential

An exact reproduction of the White House model from which LBJ preferred to give press conferences, Texas-style.

The Super Bowl

When it's time to go for "the bomb."

The Porcelain Pony

Yipee-ay-yay!! Get
along, little doody!

Incontinental Airlines

Fasten your seat belt and leave your troubles behind.

The Pit Stop

Gentlemen, start your colons!

Inflate-A-Bowl

Convenience for you, hospitality for your guests. Turn any room in your home into a guest bathroom in no time, with Inflate-A-Bowl!™ All Inflate-A-Bowl™ commodes include built-in electric pump, which inflates the heavy-gauge, puncture-resistant vinyl toilet bowl in seconds. Tongs, storage duffel included.

Good Jokes for You to Gag On!

Squirt Johnny!

It peepee on you backward! Funny for fool friend!

Volcano-oh, no!

Small little pill in commode bowl make big eruption massive overflowing when friend is sitting down on!

Ka-ka Boom!

Secret war surplus water mini-mine blow off friend ass for hearty laughing all around!

Doo-Shoes!

Look as if you "stepped in it" with both feet! Knee-high style "Doo-Boot" also is available.

Glo-doo!

Simply eat Glo-doo pill with meal. After words, secret Ingredient Radium make toidy bowl sunshine bright from doo-light! Read by doo-light!

S—t for Brains Hat.

Wear with pride on own head!

Ass-backward.

Wear for fun time.

Butt-butt.

Genuine plastic toy and conversation starter for offer cigarette to pals.

No Fake Ca-Ca!

Exceedingly comedic when friends pick up with hands! Looks resembling fake plastic "doggy doo" but is real stuff!

New Improved Classical "Whoopie Cushion"!

Add water-holder filter to air hole for realistic sound of "juicy wet one"! Add stink-perfume filter as well for horrible "pee-yoo" humor!

WET ONE   STINK   SURPRISE

Clip-on Shoe Poo!

MY NEW WHITE RUG RUIN! AIYEE! GET OUT, YOU BAGSCUM!

Good pool time fun!

In secret, blow up big lumpy turd balloon, release to float in water on top. Watch out for other bathers jump out of pool and fearful outcry!

Super Balloon!

NEW! Let go yourself! You give it the gas!

Funny cigar joke!

Cigar looks like turd! (Also smelling like!)

You can be the lives of a party.

Put big load of lumpy stinky stuff down back of own trousers! Next promenade among fellow merry makers. All persons present think you pooped!

Gag Tee Shirts!

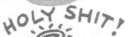

HOLY SHIT!

HOTTEST SHIT ON WHEELS

SHIT HAPPENS

CACA DE VACA

no shit.

YOU'RE NOT SHITTING ME!

MERDE! pardon my French

Seagull SPLAT!

NEW! Stick on neighbor's new car – he really crap in pants!

Save dollars! Urine develop film!

"Impossible" you say? Pee for your own self!

Lumpy Stuff!

Keep on executive desk, squeeze when tense. Feel better fast!

Memo Magnets!

Big Surprise!

No sinker Stinker! Balloon look like immense floating poop left over in bowl! Put inside for guest to find! Guaranteed too big to flush and will never sink!

BULL SHIT!

Good toy for place on office desk.

When fellow worker tells you fib, lift tail. Bull says Bullshit—and do it right on desk!

Traditional "Burning Shit Bag" trick.

1. Poop in paper bag.
2. Put poopy bag on neighbor porch.
3. Set bag on fire.
4. Ring bell, run, hide.
5. Neighbor certain to stomp foot on!

LIGHT HERE

POTTY BAG

Effluvia

I waken in a meadow
sweet. I
greet the morning new.
And then with unshod
pilgrim feet, I
step into the dew.

COLORADO PINE BRANCH COLON CLEANSER

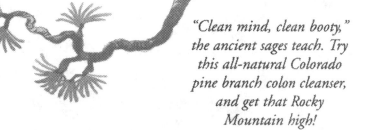

*"Clean mind, clean booty,"
the ancient sages teach. Try
this all-natural Colorado
pine branch colon cleanser,
and get that Rocky
Mountain high!*

"REAR WINDOW" WIND CHIMES

*If your all-natural, high-fiber diet consists entirely of chickpeas,
lentils, and other healthy but explosive legumes, simply strap on
our "Rear Window" wind chimes, and you shall have music
wherever you go!*

"Good Karma" toilet seats

Hand-whittled in Vermont, these "Good Karma" toilet seats are perfect for your Dharma buns! Models include:

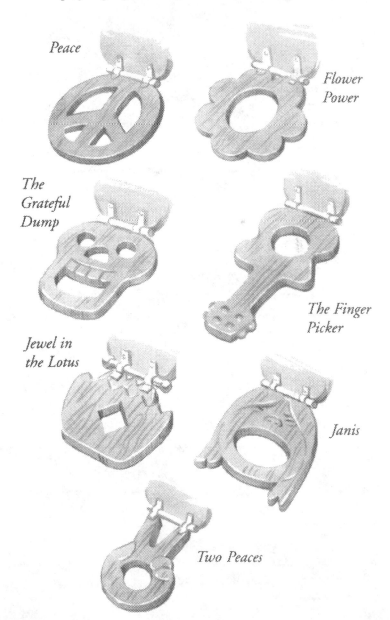

Peace

Flower
Power

The
Grateful
Dump

The Finger
Picker

Jewel in
the Lotus

Janis

Two Peaces

THE BOOK OF DUMPA YOGA

Achieve True Inner Emptiness through the Practice of Assanas and Merde-itation.

Experience for yourself the Eastern mystery of Yabyum—
"the thunder in the void"—by practicing such positions as the
ones shown below.

THE POT SQUAT

THE CURRY HURRY

THE FOOLISH MONGOOSE

THE EYE-TO-EYE

THE PIPE CLEANER

THE DIRTY SEAT

MADAME TURDETTA'S BOWL & BOXER READING

'ou Are What You Ate—the Science of Skidmarkology.

Learn the art of "fortune-telling" by interpreting the secret meanings of under-wear stains and toilet bowl leave-behinds.

(a) Trouble behind, trouble ahead. (b) You will travel soon. (c) You are of a romantic nature. (d) You will be run down by a Toyota. (e) You have a sunny disposition in spite of your hemorrhoids. (f) You are ass-ertive. (g) You are artistic. (h) You will lose a pet. (i) You are absent-minded.

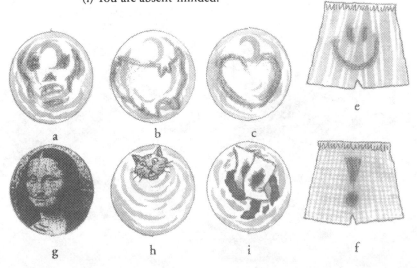

a   b   c   e

g   h   i   f

d

THE BOOK OF THE DUIDS

*What ancient secrets did they learn while
releasing the energy within?*

Builders of Dunghenge

Worshipers at the Giant's Hole

STAINED-GLASS SUNCATCHERS

*Brighten your windows with these——all personally stained by
Old World crapsmen:*

Rainbow
Buns

Brown
Comet

Rainbowl

Pooping
Angel

MAGNETO BELT

*For Better Health, Don't Feed Your Head, Feed Your Rectum!
It's hole-istic, and oh so easy, when you wear a Nature's Other
Way™ Magneto Belt! Reverse-polarity peristalsis increases vitality.*

TA-TOOTS

Nudism is healthy, pure, and natural. But even nudists like to "dress up" sometimes. That's when it's time for Ta-toots,™ the tattoos for the tushie! They're colorful, cute, and easy to apply!

BLOSSOM

PUPPY BREATH

BUTTOCK'S CHARGE

POT O' LENTILS

YIN-YANG

TAILPIPE

GO 'N' GRO

Recycle nature's bounty with the all-in-one, personal composter.

Togetherness Candle

For that air of intimacy, even during those lonely times when your loved one is far from home. Available in five organic scents (please specify): Lentil, Cabbage, Mung, Veggie-Burger, or Blackstrap Molasses.

The Runner's Friend

Nothing can take the enjoyment out of a competitive marathon—or a healthful morning jog—like "that certain feeling." Now you can "hit the wall" without having to "hit the head," and "feel the burn" without "feeling the brown," thanks to this simple, easy-to-use device. Made of all-natural, super-absorbent Spanish cork. One size fits all.

OLD-FASHIONED BATHROOM DEODORIZERS!

*They're back! Old-fashioned bathroom deodorizers! Our artisans
have handcrafted from select softwoods these "striking" reproductions of the original, traditional "de-stinkifiers." Many other uses!*

FOR A "HONEY" OF A MOVEMENT—BEE M

*Just as Royal Jelly from the hive is nature's finest rejuvenator,
Bee M, collected direct from the bums of millions of busy, buzzy
bumblebees, is nature's best laxative! Bee M is guaranteed to have
you singing, "Doo bee doo bee doo!"*

Stay "productive" in retirement. It's wonderful the way you're "holding on"—but it's a good idea to "let go" from time to time! It might even be the most exciting thing you do all day!

Prune-Mate

Auto-kathartik® dispenser mounts on wall.

Bolo Tie Pants Raiser

No more bathroom "stoop 'n' stumble," thanks to our *Bolo Tie Pants Raiser* (pat. pending).

End constipation worries!

No more straining, no more grunting! The oh-so-simple *Bowel Constrictor*™ works like a blood-pressure cuff, to apply the squeeze you need to "get the lead out." Squeezy does it! Just pump and dump!

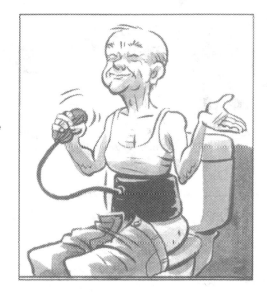

Up an' at 'Em™

Falling asleep on the toilet? Or just forgetting where you are? You need our *Up an' at 'Em*™ alarm system and spring-action ejector seat!

Fly-Gutter™ prevents embarrassing wet spots.

Record your movements in this B. M.s journal.

You'll never miss again with *Bowl-Moat*®

Handy, light-hearted, large-print fridge *Memo Magnets*® remind your family where you are.

High Cotton™ Incontinence Products

From High Cotton™ Incontinence Products, high-fashion, ultra-absorbent undergarments for all occasions. For formal wear, the classic, black-and-white "Penguin" model lets you waddle the night away! For poolside and beach wear, we recommend our "Bathing Booty" model.

Rest in Poop

Bin Loadin'

Executive

Wise Fly

Rear Window

Hole in One

Just Let It Out

Semi-Wild Thong

Fill 'er Up!

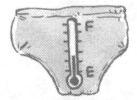

Time for a Change

Hot Tamale

Mona Turda

Grandpa's Brag Lid™

Decorate the room where you spend most of your time!

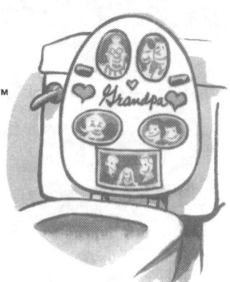

Bowl Boots®

For those delightful "second childhood" moments, when you feel you want to be in with it—washable rubber *Bowl Boots*® (open-toed model available).

SWEET SMELL OF SUCCESS

Great gifts, awards, and "leave behinds" sure to "make a big splash"!

Recognize increased employee output.

A well-received award for hunkering down behind the CEO!

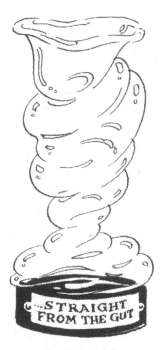

No BS! Tell it like it is!

Show 'em who knows squat!

*Words of wisdom to motivate your employees
to bear down harder!*

How to tell an undigested security from a floating loan.

High-class, handcrafted graffiti for the Executive Washroom.

A signed, framed, limited edition of the classic motivational poster "The Men's Room Guide to Success."

Coprolite Cookery
365 recipes, including the classic Army dish Shit on a Shingle, as well as Runs on a Bun, Shite on White, Excreta on Whole Wheat-a, Dump on Pump, and the trendy new Crap Suzettes.

The Big Frrrrappp!
A creationist-astronomer's alternative to the atheistic Big Bang theory. Notre Dame University's Father Kurt Fahrt, s.j., hypothesizes that the universe began when the Supreme Being accidentally "let go a wet one."

THE BIG FRRRAPPP!

Movers and Shakers
A steamy collection of anecdotes—candid "potty talk" from Washington pundits and Hollywood celebrities.

The Public Restrooms of Madison County
A nonfiction sequel.

May I Take Your Ordure?
Memoirs of a bedpan handler.

Who Moved My Shit?
The self-help book that flushes
away the small stuff. By the
author of *Who Cut the Cheese?*

We've Got Books Up the Wazoo!

What to Expect When You're Excreting
An expert suggests it's all perfectly natural.

Still Constipated After All These Years
Andy Rooney explains why he still has that look on his face.

Deeper into the Septic Tank
Erma Bombeck, one mo' time.

Rest Stop of the Gods
The riddle of Earth's geography solved—the continents are the "doo-doo piles" of ancient visitors from space.

Merder on the Orient Express
This who-dun-it? is solved by "process of elimination."

Not If I Had a Mouthful
An etiquette authority deplores the use of vulgar language.

A History of American Political Movements
Secrets from the recently discovered "logbooks" of the White House Plumbers.

What? And Leave Show Business?
A circus memoir.

BOWELS & NO BOWL

All I Really Need to Know I Learned from the "Employees Must Wash Hands Before Leaving Washroom" Sign

Hygiene for the simple-minded.

Bad Dog! Bad, Bad Dog!

Mrs. Woodhouse meets a mutt even she can't house-train.

The Slamming Shut of the American Butt

A respected academic bemoans the "uptight" attitudes of today's students.

The Golden Goose

A conservative economist recommends a massive tax break for the wealthy, "an enema for the economy that's sure to trickle down."

From a Great Height

A respected CEO recommends corporate discipline.

The Stay-Thin, All-Olestra Diet

Eat everything you can get your hands on, then blow it out your ass!

How Honorable Was My Discharge?

General Colon Bowel looks back.

Behold! A Steaming Heap of Something That Smells like Sulfur and Brimstone

Number 666 in the "Left Behind" Series.

Twice Round the Bowl and Pointed at Both Ends

An Australian bush doctor advocates the Beer and Prawns Diet.

Did I Know Pancho Villa?

A memoir by the great bandito's frequent luncheon companion.

The Big Brown One

An unflinching investigation of World War II troop movements.

Chicken Poop for the Soul

Author Dave Fisher kids the icky bestseller—but wishes he could have said "shit."

A newly discovered Sherlock Holmes mystery!

Join the famous detective as he sniffs out evil and follows the scent in *The Riddle of the Sphincter* or, "Alimentary, My Dear Watson."

Seven Habits of Highly Effective Brown-Nosers

Success Strategies When Bootlicking Isn't Enough. Another guide to doing your business by the author of *Don't Sweat the Hard Chunks* and *I'm OK, You're Full of Shit.*

Videos and DVDs—
We're positioned to get 'em
as soon as they're released!

Action-Adventure:

Hold On!, Running Scared, Don't Bother to Knock, Behind Locked Doors, The Squeeze, Backfire, Look Back in Anger, Making It, Grunt!, The Harder They Come, Every Which Way but Loose, Letting Go, The Harder They Fall, Splash, I Cover the Waterfront, The Perfect Specimen, The Corn Is Green

Comedy:

The Boom Boom Room, I Dood It, Five Easy Pieces, Yellow Submarine, The Unsinkable Molly Brown, The Paper Chase

Mystery/Suspense:

Splendor in the Grass, The Dark at the Top of the Stairs, The Blob, Who Done It? Blame it on the Bellboy

B O W E L S & N O B O W L

From our "Backlog" Video Series

The Honey House Mooners
Ed brings something special home from the sewer as an anniversary present for Trixie. Ralph mistakes it for his lunch and the fun begins!

I've Got a Pantload
Blindfolded celebrity panelists try to guess what the "mystery guest" ate for lunch.

The Fartridge Family
The band has an unexpected hit when Danny finds a new way to play the kazoo.

Dungsmoke
Chester falls through the roof of the livery stable into big trouble.

Lump unto My Feet
Anal-compulsive "table talk" by Martin Luther.

Make Room For Doody
A big couscous dinner causes plumbing problems in the Williams household.

Emission Impassible.
The White House will become the Brown House unless Mr. Briggs and the team can stop "The Enema Within."

Stardrek: The Khan of Wrath
The Enterprise is trapped in a cosmic colon, and the only exit is surrounded by Klingons!

Classic "outtakes" from *The Ed Sulliedvent Show*

Elvis below the waist—he isn't just wiggling his hips!

Angry comic Jackie Mason "moons" the host.

Señor Wences opens "de box" and finds a big "surprise" from Yawny!

Music: CDs, DVDs and BMs

A Collection of Pop's Greatest Shits, from "Doin' What Comes Natcherly" to "Oops! I Did It Again!" (includes: "Please Release Me," "Moanin' Low," "Classical Gas," and "Splish Splash"!)

Also available:

Chamber Music: Beethoven's tortured sonata *Il Constipata*; Mozart's greatest movements

NATIONAL MUSEUM O'FART

30 Centuries of Masterfeces

From Old Egypt, the throne of Pharoah Pootenkaka

Cherub with Full Diaper, by Lorenzo Evacuazione, 14th century

WHO DIDN'T FLUSH?!?

Who didn't flush?!? by Roy Lichtenschein, 20th century

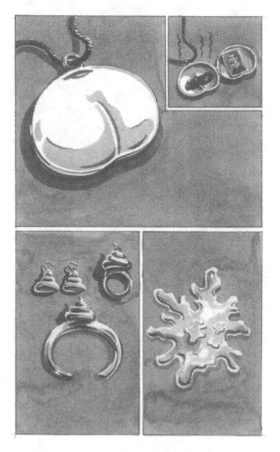

Art Dooveau "keepsake" locket
During the long engagements traditional in the Victorian era,
couples kept precious reminders of their loved ones in such
romantic lockets. Crafted of genuine phewter.

Inca "Dinka Doo"
From our pre-Columbian collection, electroplated in 18–carat
gold, the metal which the people of the Peruvian Andes knew
as "the excrement of the gods."

Bird-watcher's "trophy" brooch
A realistic "souvenir" of a rare avian sighting, crafted of fresh,
wet-looking enamel.

Turd in Space
Constipat Browncuzi's 1928 breakthrough treatment of solid and void initiated the *derrière-garde* movement.

The Stinker
French sculptor Augusht Roadapple in 1880 captured, in all its intensity, the stress and flux of modern life.

Tif-Fanny Very Stained Glass Bedpan
A painstaking reproduction of the Louis Discomfort original, in your choice of water lily or housefly designs.

Greek "Specimen" Vase
Perhaps it was this Attic amphora that inspired Keats to compose his "Ode on a Grecian's Urine"! Depicts Urea passing water (shown) and, on reverse, Hercules drinking the stale of horses, with a twist.

DooDoo in My Tutu
Edgar Degass (French, 1834–1917) had a life-long obsession with the "movements" of dancers. Our copy is bronze, and hand-wiped.

THE PRECRAPAELITES

At the tailend of the 19th century, English artists, flushed with excitement at the recent innovation of indoor plumbing, turned their talents to designing furniture, tiles, and fabrics. Their work continues to move us today.

The Butt Scarf
This enchanting design, "Meadow with Muffins," is based on the original in London's Victoria and Albutt Museum.

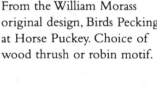

Wallpaper
From the William Morass original design, Birds Pecking at Horse Puckey. Choice of wood thrush or robin motif.

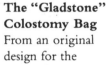

The "Gladstone" Colostomy Bag
From an original design for the Prime Minister, by "Powder" Burne-Jones.

Drapes for the Posterior
Add dramatic flair to your *derrière!* Fashioned of flashy *crap de chine.*

ASSIAN ART

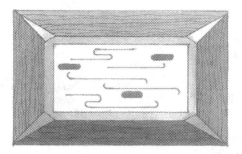

Who Make in Pool? Oyuki print by Pi Yu.

Vertical paper scroll: P'ong dynasty

Duddha Contemplating the Great Void

D'ung dynasty squat box: Richly enameled in classic "stinky pants" pattern.

Samurai letter opener: Japanese inscription reads, "Cut the Krapamaki."

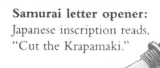

Whimsical hand–carved ivorylike Japanese netsuke, known as "Oops! So solly!"

Krapmono: Luxurious silk "swirly" pattern, features traditional sliding door.

FROM OUR BOOKSTALL

Messterpieces of Excretionism

A richly illustrated treasury of the Excretionist movement.

Cancan in the Can
by Tooloose LaDreck

Road Apples with Air Freshener
by Paul Cezanus

Outhouse at Arles
by Vincent Can Go

Surrearism

An exhaustive look back at the products of the great DooDooists and Surrearists, including Salvador Dooli, Marcel Doochamp, and Rene Excrete.

FROM OUR BOOKSTALL

Treasures of the Sistine Chapel Men's Room

Drawings, paintings and graffiti from the walls and stalls by every great artist who ever "went" there: Michelangigottago, Buttismelli, and many more.

Bass Ackwards. Oil paint on tile, by Pietro Crappi

Il Dumpio. Crayon on mirror, by Luigi Flatulenza

Putti Gone Pooty. Chalk on floor by Fece Canneloni

Shepherd Playing Crackbutt. Fresco on stall, by Alberto Tucci

Portrait of Lorenzo Crapuli. Charcoal on paper towel, by Skidmarco Undi

103

FROM OUR BOOKSTALL

The Last Days of Dumpeii

When Mount Assuvius erupted in 49 B.C., an entire civilization was "caught with its pants down."

Scatitarium

Crapqueduct with Dooditaria

CONSTIPEA   LAXITIVA

The Arch of Titass

Trajan's Colon

Fresco——
Shepherd Wiping with Sheep

The Pantion

Temple of Proctologia

Wall painting——
Warrior Centaur

FROM OUR BOOKSTALL

The Bowelhaus

A retrospective tribute to the revolutionary school of art, architecture, and design, based on the "steamlined" shape of a human turd.

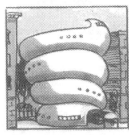

The Doodinheim Museum, NY (Frank Lloyd Shite)

Kakashtinker Center, Frankfart

Slice toaster

Fabric design— Poop in Coffee Mug

Crapplin—The Hinderturd

Locomovement

Office building, Dhartenploppandsmellitz

A Plop Art Calendar

List your daily duties in this dashing date book, which features the output of the masters of Plop!

Shit, by Robert Endiana

Toilet Paper Core,
Times Square, NY,
by Claus Oldenturd

Holy Shit!,
by Keith Hiney

CLASSIC POSTERS

The Artist's Mother, 1899, by Sir Thomas Crapper

Young Woman with Thunder Mug, 1670, by Vermeer

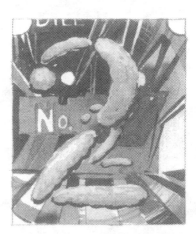

Number Two in Gold, 1928, by Charles Doomuch

CLASSIC POSTERS

La Danse de W.C., 1909, by Henri Matissue

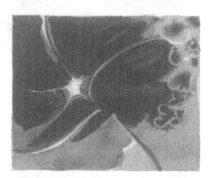

Black Anus, 1929,
by Georgia O'Keeffe

Asshole, 1970,
by Kurt Vonneguts

The Cabinet of Copro Collectibles

LIRR
PENN
STA.

John Lennon

"Leave no turd unstowed"

New!
The King was going.
The King was gone.

Own a piece of "the King's last throne"—a genuine splinter from the actual toilet seat that Elvis was sitting on when he passed! Comes with a certificate of authenticity personally initialed by Graceland hanger-on Bubba "Scatman" Yokum.

Victoria's Other Secrets

Covers and Cozies

Bring back memories of a more refined and genteel age with these genuine imitation hand-crocheted toilet seat covers and toilet paper roll cozies, similar to those adorning the WCs of Buckingham Palace, circa 1850!

Load-bearing Unmentionables

Because the ever-so-proper ladies of former times couldn't always make it to the "convenience," they wore beneath their skirts whalebone re-enforced, load-bearing Unmentionables! Now you can, too!

H.G. Wells' Perpetual Anti-Contstipation Machine!

Designed to continuously project the over-loaded Victorian bowel back into the past, rendering defecation itself unnecessary!

The Gentleman's Water Closet Companion

A smudgy reprint of the naughty joke book Prince Albert kept in his own private loo. A treasury of British toilet humor for those who treasure British toilet humor!

Bonus——printed on soft, strong, absorbent pulp paper, with plenty of blank pages in back for "emergency" purposes.

From the Golden Age of Bedpan Alley

Vintage Shee-eet Music for the Men's Room Quartet

"There's a lot you can learn from poop."

—Toshiko Sunanda, curator,
Excrement Exhibit, Tokyo Science Museum, 2001

Today, the very best people are collecting and displaying the rare, precious, and beautiful objects scientists call "coprolites"— but we call "doo-dads." Now you, too, can acquire and display a breathtaking array of these prehistoric fossilized dinosaur feces, simply by joining our exclusive Poot-of-the-Month Club!

Dungasaurus (or "Thunderbutt")

Rhubarb-eating Dreckadon; Silent but Deadly Craptor

It's My Hobby!

For the model railroader! A colorful, realistic selection of HO-scale "thoughtless turdlettes." Scatter them on the tracks to indicate that some passengers did not heed the on-board request to "refrain from flushing the toilet while the train is in the station!"

Make Your Own Shit in a Bottle! Amaze your friends with your crapsmanship! Kit contains bottle, cork and simple, easy-to-follow instructions.

Caca-tures!

She's the cutie on doody. She's the Ooops! Girl. She's Betty Poop!

Classic 1937 cartoon "Caca-tures" reproduced in authentic Crappalite™ Styrene.

New! Animation cells from WWII poopaganda films. Rare, precious, and reeking of authenticity.

Brick, personally passed in a moment of frustrated creativity by architect Frank Lloyd Shite, (with genuine forged certificate of authenticity).

Tinseltown Memorabilia!

Lassie's Passies

Precious souvenirs of the beloved movie pooch! Available in sateen-lined presentation case, with certificate of authenticity personally signed by "Scooper Man" Leech, "the celebrity dog-walker."

Custom-made "Flaming Asshole" cigarette lighter, custom-made for beloved movie mogul Matty Symonds, reproduced by permission of the asstate.

Perfect in every detail!

Replica of Eva Gabor's Incontinence Diaper Pin, marked Cartier, with certificate of semi-authenticity.

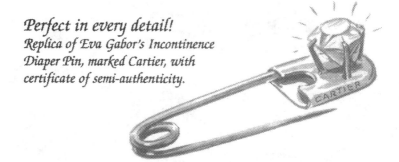

Sports memorabilia that's guaranteed to "hit" the "fan"!

A LeRoy Neiman-ish fine art sports print
Arnie Drops a Doozie: The golfing legend in action, sinking an impossibly long poot in the sand trap beside the eighth green at Augusta.

For "Bleacher Bums" Only!
Vintage Scatch 'n' Sniff baseball cards, featuring Walter "Boob-Boom" Beck, Jim Bottomley, Harry "Stinky" Davis, Tommy "Buckshot" Brown, Hugh "Duffmeir" Duffy, Henry "Heinie" Manush.

But what is this? ha! oh, ho! how the devil came I by this? Do you call this what-the-cat-left-in-the-malt, filth, dirt, dung, dejection, foecal matter, excrement, stercoration, sir-reverence, ordure, second-hand meats, fumets, stronts, scybal, or spyathe? 'Tis Hibernean saffron, I protest...and so much for this time. Selah. Let us drink!

—Rabelais, Gargantua and Pantagruel
(Urquart-Motteux translation)